Lorentz Transformation

for high school students

> What I say & do today,
> decide my future & define me.
>
> 今日的言行，造就明日的我。

By: Sauce Huang

作者：黄酱

Order this book online at www.trafford.com
or email orders@trafford.com

Most Trafford titles are also available at major online book retailers.

Printed in the United States of America.

ISBN: 978-1-4907-4742-2 (sc)
ISBN: 978-1-4907-4744-6 (hc)
ISBN: 978-1-4907-4743-9 (e)

Library of Congress Control Number: 2014917102

Trafford rev. 09/23/2014

North America & international
toll-free: 1 888 232 4444 (USA & Canada)
fax: 812 355 4082

Dedication

To Jo-En, Paul and Jay

> What I say & do today,
> decide my future & define me.
>
> 今日的言行，造就明日的我。

Catalog:

Appendixes

Lorentz Transformation

for high school students

What I say & do today,
decide my future & define me.

今日的言行，造就明日的我。

Preface

Newton's first law of motion is often stated as followings:

An object at rest stays at rest and an object in motion stays in motion with the same speed and in the same direction unless it is acted upon by an unbalanced force.

When you apply this law of motion to the real world you may find the difference between a theory and an experiment.

Here is what I experienced in year 1970. At first I thought a cup on a table was rest because the table provided enough upward force to balance the gravitational force. Then I thought about the self-spin of earth and understood that the cup received an accelerating force from earth via the friction force in between the bottom of the cup and the table so that it was circling the axis of self-spin at almost equal speed. And then I thought about the four seasons caused by the fact that earth was moving around the sun and that changed my idea about the almost equal speed of the cup.

After that I thought about tons of collisions, actions of the kinetic forces, caused by the hits from some air particles and tons of photons. So many collisions per second, even per nanosecond, that change the motions of electrons in the cup.

I was unable to see the electrons but did I finish all the possible forces I knew? No, not yet. The reason electrons are not leaving the cup was due to the electronic force, the one keeps electrons circling their nuclei was the attraction force between positive charges and negative charges. You will think, that should be all the forces relative to the cup. But I did some more imagination.

While electrons within the cup running around and photons getting in and out of the cup, I could sense that, nuclei in the cup were not stationary.

They were vibrating or just waving, jolting and randomly moving. They might jerk or sit still once in a while too. All the motions of nuclei were of tiny scales.

But I was sure that with moving electrons around them, which changed the electronic field wrapping them, nuclei would not just sit there. That meant every part of the cup was breathing with the environment! The whole cup! At that moment, the cup was a kind of alive to me. I still remember that wonderful moment of my life, now and here.

To enjoy physics we all need some imagination. Now, open your imagination and I will try to show you the key point of the modern relativity theory, the Lorentz Transformation. I will focus on the theory and hope you could find some way to verify the theory.

I am sorry that the book is so tiny that it does not have a book ridge. I really like it to have a book ridge. That is the only reason I added appendixes to give it a book ridge. Please ignore the appendixes if you do not read Chinese.

Thanks for your understanding, I appreciate it.

Sauce Huang
September, 2014 in Redmond, WA 98052

1. The velocity of Light

The first knowledge relative to Lorentz Transformation (LT) is the velocity of light. A velocity has a speed and a direction.

Scientists already proved that the speed of light is independent to the speed of the source of light. For sources with low speed, you may refer to Sagnac effect (1913 by George Sagnac) and for sources with high speed you may refer to the experiment reported on 8/20/1964 by T. Alvager, F. Farley, J. Kjellman and I. Wallin.

1-1. How about the velocity?

Let me start this knowledge from a simple setup. Let a train moves at a constant speed v along a straight segment of railroad. I will need your help to point a flashlight to outside of the train from an open window and let the flashlight perpendicular to the plane containing the frame of that window.

Then I want you to turn the flashlight on and off once in the night time so that there should be a ray of light rushes out into the dark space. Now, I need you to imagine the speed of the ray and the direction of it.

About the speed, scientists already assure us that the speed of photons will not be influenced by the speed of the flashlight so that it will not be $(c^2+v^2)^{(1/2)}$. The speed of photons is a constant c, in vacuum.

I hope you understand this ugly way to display the wrong speed of $(c^2+v^2)^{(1/2)}$. The symbol of "^" is to represent the function of exponents, c^2 is for the square of c and $(c^2+v^2)^{(1/2)}$ is for the positive square root of (c^2+v^2).

How about the direction of the ray? Let me ask you to turn the flashlight on and off when you see the center line of a road perpendicular to the railroad. In that situation I will say the direction of that ray is away from the train and along the center line of that road. Do you think so?

I hope you do. Then, as the middle train on the diagram of next page, I will assume that I already put a huge mirror face to the train at the center line of the road about 100 meter away to reflect the ray back to the train.

Now, please imagine this situation and decide if the returning ray will hit the center point of the front circular, square or rectangular surface of your flashlight.

If your answer is will not, which is what I believe, then your idea is showed on the bottom train of the diagram on next page. If your answer is yes then I will talk about it later.

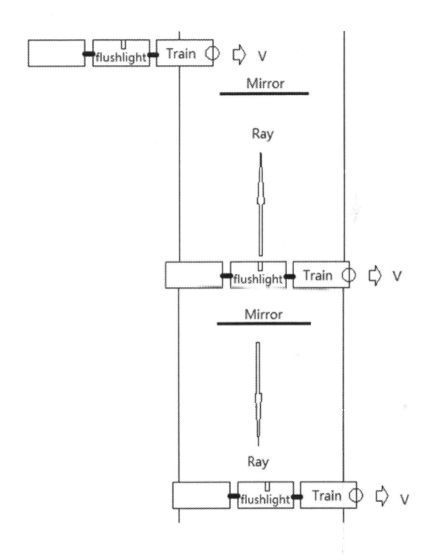

1-2. A Natural Selection

If you select that the return ray will not hit the center point of the face of your flashlight then the velocity of light is independent to the velocity of the source of light. I call it the natural selection of the velocity of light and mark that kind of ray by a Cn vector.

A Cn vector will go by its own direction. No matter how fast the source of light moves or how fast the source of light spins, a Cn vector will represent the speed c and the direction like the ray is emitted from a stationary source in the universe.

When technology is good enough to record nanosecond and nanometer accurately, scientists could use the setup in 1-1 to design an experiment. I hope that Cn vectors will be verified.

Under the definition of Cn vectors, the figure 39-6 on page 1200 of "University Physics" tenth edition by Young & Freedman published in year 2000 (Book 1) will need some modifications.

Under the definition of Cn vectors, the figure\38-5 on page 963 of "Fundamentals of Physics extended" fifth edition by Halliday, Resnick and Walker published in year 1997 (Book 2) will also need some modifications and the proved result after the modification will be "time acceleration", not "time dilation" any more.

1-3. The Mainstream Selection

Yes, logically speaking, a ray may adjust its direction according to the velocity of the source of light while maintaining its speed c. Why? Because scientists don't know a ray thoroughly yet.

I mark that kind of rays by Cm vectors. This kind of vector is a confusing vector. It will partially follow the operational rules of vectors. The Cm vectors will follow the operational rule for directions but not the operational rule for scales.

Yes, regarding following the operational rules of vectors, a Cn vector is worse than a Cm vector because a Cn vector will ignore both of the scale and direction of the velocity vector of the source of light.

The mainstream selection in physics is that the return ray in the section 1-1 will hit the center point of the face of your flashlight. That means Cm vectors is the choice of most scientists of physics in representing a ray of light wave.

Remember that, neither Cn vectors nor Cm vectors are mathematical vectors. Both of them violet the operational rules of mathematical vectors. They are for physics only.

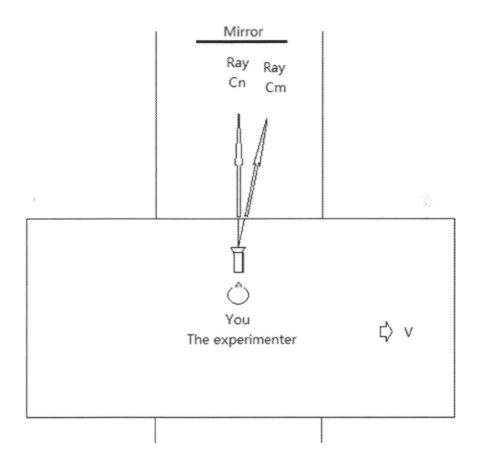

I believe that someday scientists should be able to put this train experiment into test. When that day comes you or your children may see the result of the competition between model of Cn vectors and model of Cm vectors.

1-4. The Cm vectors

Since photons is an important object of physics let me talk more about the character of Cm vectors.

Mathematically, when scientists decide the direction of a ray emitting from a moving source at constant velocity V, it will be like the combined vector, the Cc vector, in the following diagram.

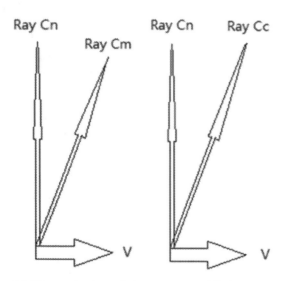

V, The velocity of the source of light

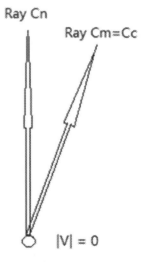

Spinning source of light

The length of Cc is $|Cc| = (c^2+v^2)^{(1/2)}$, where $|V| = v$. The length of Cn vectors and Cm vectors are $|Cn|=|Cm|= c$.

As you can tell, when $|V| > 0$, we always have $|Cm| < |Cc|$ but the direction of Cm is always the same as it of Cc.

The idea of mainstream professors of physics makes photons behave in between of independent (the spped) and dependent (the direction) to the velocity of the source of light.

The photons in a ray will follow the direction of vector Cc, which is the direction of combined vector from vectors of Cc and V. That is the dependent portion, the direction of photons depend on the velocity of the source of light.

But photons in a ray will not always accept the speed portion of the vector Cc. When $|V| = 0$, we do have $|Cc| = |Cm| = c$ but when $|V| > 0$, $|Cc| > |Cm| = c$.

I hope you have a clear picture of how the velocity of the source of light influence the behavior of photons it emits. We don't know which model of Cn and Cm is matching the nature, the fact, but currently most professors of physics believe that Cm vectors is the right model.

The model of Cn vectors let the velocity of light totally independent of the velocity of the source of light.

2. Michelson Morley experiment

Scientists use the model of Cm to explain the famous Michelson Morley experiment (MMX, 1887) so that the null result of MMX causes scientists to rely on Lorentz Transformation (LT) for a logical explanation of MMX.

However, following the model of Cn vectors, you will understand that when the reflecting ray returns back to the beam splitter, either in the figure 37-16 on page 1154 of (Book 1) or figure 36-45 on page 927 of (Book 2), it will not reach the center point of the splitter as the model of Cm vectors expected.

When the apparatus turns as designed procedure of MMX, the model of Cn vectors shows the reflecting ray and the penetrating ray will meet at the center area of the beam splitter at 45 degree and 225 degree only. That means, within Cn model, MMX is self-explained to expect for the null result so long as the area around the center point of the light bulb is flat.

21

The minor experimental results in all MMX related experiments were due to the curvature of the light bulb.

If you like, you may study the MMX with this new point of view base on the model of Cn vectors.

According to the Cn model, when the penetrating ray returns back to the center area of the beam splitter, it will not combine with the original reflecting ray. It will combine with the reflecting ray of another emitting ray which is emitted from a location away from the center point of the light bulb.

A diagram of how the MMX can be explained properly is provided on page 114 of the book "Special Relativity of Roses & Happiness".

http://bookstore.trafford.com/Products/SKU-000959590/Special-Relativity-of-Roses--Happiness.aspx

You may refer to it if you like to dig into more details of the MMX. But for the purpose of this book, I will stop talking about MMX and introduce LT in as much details as I can offer.

3. Lorentz Transformation

Scientists in the mainstream of physics use LT to explain the null result of MMX. This is definitely a valid option so long as LT is well learned, at least, as good as what you will learn from this book.

In high school physics, students do not study LT because LT is beyond what people need to handle their daily affairs. There are too many practical subjects in physics and if some further knowledge of physics should be put into high school physics it would be solar energy, nuclear physics and quantum theory. I believe that the further knowledge for high school physics will not include LT because the main purpose of study for most students is for a better job, at least, more opportunity of employment and LT will not help.

However, if you study physics in university then you will have to learn LT. This book will explain the foundation of LT very clearly for you.

3-1. Galilean Transformation

First of all, what relative to LT and may be useful for high school students is the simple Galilean Transformation (GT).

This is the third item relative to LT which I have mentioned about up to now. The velocity of light and MMX are important in learning LT but GT is the soul of this book and the father of LT.

As a proverb states, like father like son, to understand LT well you must learn GT thoroughly. I said GT is simple however there are two hidden properties of GT can confuse students easily.

Let me show you both of them.

3-1-1. Two 3-dimensional Cartesian coordinates

In GT, there are two 3-dimensional Cartesian coordinates to represent the space portion of frame S and frame S' respectively. The frame S' moves at constant velocity V relative to S, in the common positive direction of their collinear horizontal axes, the x'-axis and the x-axis.

25

In GT and LT, scientists assume that the y-axis and z-axis of S are parallel to the y'-axis and z'-axis of S' respectively with same positive direction, like upward for y-axis and y'-axis. Scientists also assume that t'= t when the origins of S and S' coincide. Let me use Po to represent the origin point of S and Po' for S'.

If observers in S report space-time coordinates (t, x, y, z) for an event Eg and observers in S' report space-time coordinates (t', x', y', z') for the same event Eg then how are these two sets of numbers related? To relate these two reported coordinates is the main purpose of GT and LT. According to GT the relation will be (t', x', y', z') = (t, x-vt, y, z).

3-1-2. t'= t

The first equation of GT is t'= t. To Mr. Galilei the formula of time is theoretically simple if scientists let event Eg happen at time Tg and location Pg then think about it.

If scientists assume there are observers everywhere in S and S' then they can ask the observer in S at Pg to report event time t=Tg and ask the observer in S' at Pg to report event time t'=Tg to get the natural result of t'= t. It's simple and it explains that GT is theoretically correct.

However, practically speaking, it is impossible to arrange an observer for some possible event like "a bullet hits a flying bird" because observers are unable to fly along with the bird and it would be too dangerous to be that observer.

If GT is not practical then scientists need a practical solution for relativity and that is one of the reasons why LT was so welcomed by professors of physics when it showed up around the end of nineteenth century.

3-1-3. x'= x-vt

The next equation of GT is $x'= x-vt$ --- (1). Because $y'= y$ and $z'= z$ are very obviously correct, the learning of GT will end after you understand the equation (1).

Now, I will need your imagination once again.

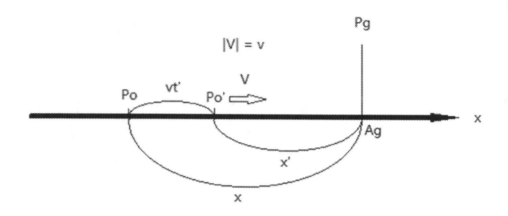

Let Ag be the project of Pg to the x-axis then x' is related to the distance of two points Po' and Ag.

We have either x'=Po'Ag or x'= -Po'Ag, it depends on if Ag is located at the right side or left side of Po' and x=PoAg or x= -PoAg. The last item PoPo' is decided by the moving point Po'. When observers in S' record event time t', the distance of PoPo' is v|t'| so that PoPo'=vt' or PoPo'= -vt'.

To combine the possible situations into a valid equation we need help of some diagrams like the one above.

According to that diagram, if Po-Po'-Ag or Po-Po'=Ag we have Po'Ag= PoAg-PoPo' and Po'Ag= x', PoAg= x with PoPo'= vt' so that x'= x-vt'. Since in GT, we have t'= t so that the equation (1), x'= x-vt is true for these two situations.

In case of Po-Ag-Po', Ag=Po-Po' or Ag-Po-Po' I need you to use the same diagram with a little bit of imagination to move the project point Ag (of event point Pg) to new locations. You will find out the relations is Po'Ag= -PoAg+ PoPo', Po'Ag=PoAg+PoPo' and Po'Ag=PoAg+PoPo' respectively. All of the relationships are equal to x'= x-vt' and (1) is true.

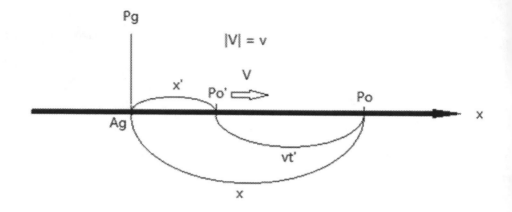

How about when t'<0 where Po' is approaching Po? Could you figure out x'= x-vt base on above diagram?

For the situation of Po=Po' we have t'=t=0 and x'=x so that the equation x'= x-vt is true. Now, we have considered all of possible situations of GT.

Do you think GT is mathematically correct even if the time equation, t'= t, is hard to prove in the real world?

3-2. Length Contraction

Lorentz Transformation (LT) let observer O stay at the origin of S and observer O' at the origin of S' so that LT can be more practical than GT. The starting point of LT is a hypothesis of length contraction. The hypothesis suggests that if O' use a ruler to measure two points on the x'-axis then the 1 unit length of the ruler will shrink to $(1/\gamma)$ unit so that the measured result will enlarge by the factor of γ in S'.

However, both of S and S' use same unit like (meter/second) for velocity and it is very important that in LT both of O' and O know that O' moves at velocity V relative to O.

That means O' moves to the positive x-axis direction at speed v is a fact to both of O and O'. If we apply the γ factor to GT, then, the distance of two points measured in S' will be enlarged to γ times of the measurement for the same two points in S. Are you ready?

3-3. The Spatial Equation

Let me write the equation (1), $x' = x-vt$, and apply the length contraction hypothesis to (1).

The variables at right side of (1) are reported by O for the distance of two points Po'and Ag with PoAg-PoPo' while the left side, x', is reported by O' for the same distance between Po' and Ag directly; we should have $x' = \gamma(x-vt)$ ---(2) under the length contraction.

3-4. The Time Equation

Since the length contraction hypothesis applies to the direction of x' axis (moving on x axis) only, we should have $y' = y$ and $z' = z$ in LT. How about the time equation?

I believe that Mr. Lorentz found his time equation by combining the spatial equation of LT and the spatial equation of inverse LT. If he did so, that action would make LT a useless transformation of $(t', x', y', z') = (t, x, y, z)$.

But I will not assume that was the way Mr. Lorentz found his time equation of LT. I will assume that he found it by some hint of nature. I will let the time equation of LT be an independent equation. It is $t' = \gamma(t-(vx/c^2))$ ---(3)

Actually, the equation (2) is not perfectly accurate when Mr. Lorentz applied his hypothesis to GT. However, in this book, I will not discuss the detail of that issue. I will introduce LT by itself, without any background check on it.

That means, I will start to explain the details of equations (2) and (3) in LT to you. Most scientists of physics accept LT as true because they believe that LT can explain MMX under the model of Cm vectors.

3-5. Equation (2) and (3) in LT

Let me combine (2) and (3) by (2)+v(3), then we will get the following equation $x = \gamma(x'+vt')$ ---(4) in LT. The key equation to get equation (4) is $1/(\gamma^2) = (1-(v^2/c^2))$. It is complicated because γ is complicated. The symbol γ is named Lorentz factor and it is $\gamma = 1/(1-(v^2/c^2))^{(1/2)}$.

33

Now, let us compare the (2) and (4) within LT. In (2) and (4), $|x'|$ is the distance of Po'Ag measured by O' and $|x|$ is the distance of PoAg measured by O. We also know that, $v|t|$ is the distance of PoPo' measured by O so that the only measurement we have not defined now is $v|t'|$. Let me explain $v|t'|$ step by step for you.

First of all, let me write (2) to show you the distance of Po'Ag in S is not measured directly. From the right side of (2), $x'= \gamma(x-vt)$, the distance of Po'Ag is calculated by $|PoAg-PoPo'|$ in S. Because Ag is a fixed point, O can measure the distance PoAg easily. But Po' is always moving, how does O measure PoPo'?

The key point is that the location of Po' can be marked on x-axis at the time the event happens, I name it Pe for the purpose of clarity.

The event time may be reported differently by O and O' but there is only one time that the event occurs and that is the time the location of Po' should be marked, as Pe.

O and O' may use different kind of rulers but they should measure the same two points, Po and Pe.

Since Po' left Po at time $t' = t = 0$, so that when O records the event Eg at time t, to O, the distance between Po and Pe should be vt if event time is positive. For negative event time t, to O, Po' need the time period $|t|$ to move from Pe to Po so that the distance between Pe and Po is $-vt$. To O, the distance PoPe$= v|t|$ is always correct.

That means the distance PePo is measured at quite the same way by O', as PoPe$=v|t'|$, because O' knows the same setup of LT as O knows. Since the same distance between Po and Pe is measured by O as $v|t|$ and measured by O' as $v|t'|$, according to the length contraction hypothesis, in LT, we should have $v|t'| = \gamma \, v|t|$.

3-6. Equation (2) and (4) in LT

We will compare (2) and (4) in LT for three points Po, Pe and Ag. Let's look into the absolute mark for $v|t|$ and $v|t'|$ first. We know that $v|t|$ is the distance of PoPe measured by O so that O must decide the t for Pe. That means there is another event that O must record besides the event Eg. Which is the location of the Po' point. One thing is for sure, that is when O sees Po' at the negative side of x-axis, then t must be negative because before Po' reach Po, both of t and t' are negative, so $t < 0$. Yes, in that situation, $t' < 0$ as well. When O sees Po' locates at the positive side of the x-axis then $t > 0$ and $t' > 0$ because after Po' passes Po, both of t and t' are positive. Since t' and t are always on the same side relative to Po, we can write the relationship of $v|t'| = \gamma v|t|$ into a simple equation that $vt' = \gamma vt$. When O sees Po' right at Po, we have $t' = t = 0$.

In (2) we have $x' = \gamma(x - vt)$ and in (4) we have $x = \gamma(x' + vt')$ so that (2)+(4) in LT can derive $x' + x = \gamma(x + x') - \gamma(vt - vt')$.

36

Let me move $\gamma(x+x')$ to the left side and let γvt replace vt' then we will have $(x'+x)(1-\gamma)=(-\gamma vt)(1-\gamma)$ ---(5) in LT.

In (5), if $\gamma=1$, then we have v=0 and the LT is a trivial transformation (t', x', y', z') = (t, x, y, z).

If $\gamma>1$ then x'+x= -γvt, that is x'= -x- γvt ---(6). Let me rewrite (2) to the (7) as x'= γx- γvt ---(7) then combine them as (7)-(6) in LT, we will get 0=x($\gamma+1$) ---(8). In the equation (8), since ($\gamma+1$) > 0, we have x=0.

That means if $\gamma>1$ then x = 0 in LT. If x = 0 (3) will be t'= γt and (2) will be x'= - γvt so that LT will be a transformation of (t', x', y', z') = (γt, - γvt, y, z) for events locating at Po only.

From equation (5) we proved that LT is either a trivial transformation or LT can be used for events locate at Po only and the time equation for those events is t'= γt, not the t'= t/ γ as claimed by Special Relativity.

That means mathematically speaking, when $v = 0$, LT is a trivial transformation $(t', x', y', z') = (t, x, y, z)$ for all events. When $v > 0$, LT is limited for events locating at Po only and the transformation is $(t', x', y', z') = (\gamma t, -\gamma vt, y, z)$.

It looks a lot simpler than the LT in most text books. Do you like it?

3-7. Mathematical physics

This chapter 3 includes only high school mathematics and the reasoning steps are not difficult to most students.

Hope this new face of LT can be tested by scientists of physics soon. In the last chapter I will talk about an important experiment of relativity and introduce a new transformation named Distance Transformation (DT).

4. Ives-Stilwell experiment (ISX)

The Ives-Stilwell experiment (ISX) is an experiment related to Doppler effect. The formula (18-53) on the page 440 of (Book 2) for Doppler effect is better than the formula (21-17) on the page 658 of (Book 1) for Doppler effect because in (Book 1) the symbol for the velocity of a listener L is comingled with the speed of it.

4-1. A non-stop Express Train

An express train will not stop at tiny stations. If you are a passenger waiting at platform of a tiny station then you may experience the Doppler effect of sound wave and light wave when you hear and watch an express train passing by the platform at constant speed, in and out of the station.

If we let the fd to represent the detected frequency, fs for the frequency of the source wave, Vw for the velocity of the wave, Vd for the velocity of the detector and Vs for the velocity of the source of wave then Doppler effect is:

$$fd = ((|Vw-Vd|)/(|Vw-Vs|))fs \text{ ---}(9)$$

But besides the Doppler effect you may find another effect.

4-2. The Speed of the Train

You may find out the speed of the train, v, is faster when it approaches the station than when it leaves the station.

This phenomenon is a common experience to people and it is an implication of an experimental version of GT named Distance Transformation (DT). Beside this basic application of DT, you may find the explanation of a common, but normally ignored, fact that the speed of light which running into our eyes are measured unlimited fast by our brain.

You may refer to page 110 and 111 of the book "Special Relativity of Roses & Happiness" for more detail if you like to know this interesting fact.

According to the equations of DT on page 148 of "SPEAK CHINESE with APA", the approaching speed of the train is measured as $(c/(c-v))v$ and the leaving speed of the train is measured as $(c/(c+v))v$, for one dimensional motion.

This can be put for test by experiments. However, in this book I will make an easy job to verify DT. All scientists of physics need to do is to collect the raw data of all experiments related to Ives-Stilwell experiment and do one comparison regarding equation (9).

4-3. When $|Vd| = 0$

When $|Vd| = 0$, the (9) will reduce to $fd = (|Vw|/(|Vw-Vs|))fs$ and if we look at the wavelength of the wave and let wd be detected wavelength and ws be the wavelength of the source wave then the equation will be:

$wda = (1-(|Vs|/|Vw|))ws$ ---(10) when the source of wave approaches detector, and it will be:

$wdl = (1+(|Vs|/|Vw|))ws$ ---(11) when the source of wave leaves detector.

This is the situation of Ives-Stilwell experiment. As you may notice, if we average these two detected wavelengths the result will be the original wave length, (wda+wdl)/2 = ws. The experiment changed the speed of the source of light wave and recorded each pair of the wda and wdl then they calculated the average length of each pair of wavelengths to compare them with the wavelength of the source, ws.

They found out, the faster the source moved, the bigger the difference between ws and the average wavelength.

4-4. ISX and Special Relativity (SR)

According to Special Relativity (SR), $t' = t/\gamma$. Since there will be time dilation in S', the period per cycle will be enlarged in S' so that the frequency of the light wave will reduce from fs to fs/γ. The (10) and (11) become

wdas = (1-(|Vs|/|Vw|)) γws ---(12) the source approaches and
wdls = (1+(|Vs|/|Vw|)) γws ---(13) the source leaves detector.

4-5. ISX and DT

According to DT, the speed of the source of light wave will increase when the source approaches detector and vice versa.

$wdad = (1-((c/(c-v))v/|Vw|))$ ws ---(14) the source approaches
$wdld = (1+((c/(c+v))v/|Vw|))$ ws ---(15) the source leaves the detector.

4-6. (12) & (13) or (14) & (15)

In (12) & (13), wdas & wdls are larger than wda & wdl; but in (14) & (15) wdad & wdld are smaller than wda & wdl. If scientists of physics could get raw data of ISX they will find out which set of equations matches most ISX data.

4-7. Conclusion

In the chapter 1, I asked professors of physics for designing experiments when technology could measure nanosecond and nanometer accurately.

The experiments are to decide if the Cn vector model for the velocity of light matches the fact or the Cm vector model for the velocity of light matches the nature.

In the chapter 3, I proved that when $v > 0$ LT is valid for the events happen at the origin point of S only, and for those events, LT is $(t', x', y', z') = (\gamma t, -\gamma v t, y, z)$. When $v = 0$, LT is $(t', x', y', z') = (t, x, y, z)$ for all events.

If you check C-11 of the book "Special Relativity of Roses & Happiness" you will find out its explanation for LT is wrong . However its proof of "LT is trivial" is correct. That book is at:

https://www.tatepublishing.com/bookstore/book.php?w=978-1-63063-908-2

In this chapter, I ask scientists of physics for checking the raw data of any experiment related to Ives-Stilwell experiment to verify if SR is correct or DT is correct, when they have time. Hope you will be able to see the result.

Appendixes

I.   APA

APA is the first step of my dream to promote an international language. APA stands for Auxiliary Phonetic Alphabet. The difference between APA and IPA (International Phonetic Alphabet) is that APA will merge similar pronunciations in IPA into same symbols so long as the mixing of those symbols will not cause any confusing to communication.

For example, the IPA for Chinese pronunciation of b, d, g and ds are p, t, k and ts. Because before Pinyin was drafted on 2/12/1956, approved on 2/11/1958, used by western publications in 1979, adopted by International Organization for Standardization (ISO) in 1982 and legalized in 2001 the pronunciation of Mandarin was more like that.

However, after so many years of promoting Pinyin and learning English I believe that the actual way Chinese people pronounce Mandarin or Putonghua must have changed quite a lot. I started APA from simplify Pinyin.

I-1. APA and Pinyin

APA phonetic symbols are prepared for an auxiliary phonetic system. It is very close to Pinyin system with the following differences:

1. z(ㄗ),c(ㄘ), s(ㄙ), and j(ㄐ), q(ㄑ), x(ㄒ) are represented as "ds", "ts", "s", and "dsi", "tsi", "si" respectively in APA.
2. zh(ㄓ), ch(ㄔ), sh(ㄕ), r(ㄖ), and e(ㄜ), er(ㄦ), ü(ㄩ), ao(ㄠ) are represented as "dR", "tR", "sR", "R", and "E", "ER", "yu", "au" respectively in APA.
3. All the lazy vowels, like the "e" in front of "n" and "ng" or the "i" after "ds", "ts", "s", and "dR", "tR", "sR", "R" are all omitted in APA.

The English portion of APA has four additional vowels and nine additional consonants:

4. u(up) - A, i(it) - I, oo(book) - U, a(cat) - ae;
   the "a" in a(about) is the same as E,
5. j(just) - dZ, ch(chip) - tZ, sh(she) - sZ,
   s(vision) - Z,
6. th(the) - D, th(thin) - T.
7. v(vision) – v, z(zoo) – z, r(run) – r

The "r" is different from "R". The semi-vowel "y" is normally represented by "j" in English. Because of this change in Pinyin, the English word "you" will have to use "iu" to represent it. Why? Because "yu" is occupied by "ü" in Pinyin.

There is no such pronunciation as "iu" in Chinese, but it is in Taiwanese.

I put each of the five symbols for the tones in Chinese at the end of each syllable. In Chinese, it is at the end of each word because all Chinese words are single syllable. However, in Pinyin the symbols for the tones are put on top of one vowel, not at the end of a word.

1(So)–" ^ ", 2(MiSo)–" / ", 3(Do)–" v ", 4(SoDo)–" \ " and 5(Re)–" - ".

Phonetic Table

B (Bopomofo), P (Pinyin), A (APA)

B	ㄅ	ㄆ	ㄇ	ㄈ	ㄉ	ㄊ	ㄋ	ㄌ
P	b	p	m	f	d	t	n	l
A	b	p	m	f	d	t	n	l

B	ㄍ	ㄎ	ㄏ		(ㄐ	ㄑ	ㄒ)
P	g	k	h		(j	q	x)
A	g	k	h		(ds	ts	s)

B	ㄓ	ㄔ	ㄕ	ㄖ	ㄗ	ㄘ	ㄙ
P	zh	ch	sh	r	z	c	s
A	dR	tR	sR	R	ds	ts	s

B	ㄚ	ㄛ	ㄜ	ㄝ	ㄞ	ㄟ	ㄠ	ㄡ
P	a	o	e	e	ai	ei	ao	ou
A	a	o	E	e	ai	ei	au	ou

B	(ㄢ)	ㄣ	(ㄤ)	ㄥ	ㄦ	ㄧ	ㄨ	ㄩ
P	(an)	n	(ang)	ng	er	y i	w u	ü
A	(an)	n	(ang)	ng	ER	y i	w u	yu

English word:	cup	hit	book	cat	very	red	zoo	you
Key letter	u	i	oo	a	v	r	z	you
APA letter	A	I	U	ae	v	r	z	iu

English word:	judge	church	ship	vision	this	thin
Key letter	j	ch	sh	s	th	th
APA letter	dZ	tZ	sZ	Z	D	T

* Tone marks

	1	2	3	4	5	6	7
Bopomofo		/	v	\			
Pinyin	-	/	v	\			
APA	^	/	v	\	-	v-	>
pitch level	Mi	ReMi	Do	MiDo	Do#	DoDo#	Re
active mood	So	MiSo	Do	SoDo	Re	DoRe	Mi

I-2. APA 表

APA 音标是一种辅助音标，和拼音非常接近，只有以下不同：

1. z(ㄗ),c(ㄘ), s(ㄙ),和 j(ㄐ), q(ㄑ), x(ㄒ) 在 APA 里头分别用 ds, ts, s, 和 dsi, tsi, si 来表示。
2. zh(ㄓ), ch(ㄔ), sh(ㄕ), r(ㄖ), 和 e(ㄜ), er(ㄦ), ü(ㄩ), ao(ㄠ) 在 APA 里头分别用 dR, tR, sR, R, 和 E, ER, yu, au 来表示。

49

3. 普通话里头的懒韵母,好比在 n 和 ng 前面的 "e" 和在 ds, ts, s, 与 dR, tR, sR, R, 後面的"i" ，在 APA 里头一律省略。

APA 在英语的部分有 4 个不同的韵母，9 个不同的声母：

4. u(up) - A, i(it) - I, oo(book) - U, a(cat) - ae; 而 a(about) – E 是相同的,
5. j(just) - dZ, ch(chip) - tZ, sh(she) - sZ, s(vision) - Z,
6. th(the) - D, th(thin) - T. v(vision) – v, z(zoo) – z，r(run) – r。

r 和 R 不相同而半韵母 "y" 在美语常用 "j" 来代表。因为拼音这个改变，英文字 "you" 就必须用 "iu" 来代表。为什么呢？因为 "yu" 已经被拼音的 "ü" 佔用。

在中文，沒有 "iu" 这个发音，但是在台语里头有。

普通话的 5 个声调符号，我放到每一个音节的後面； 在中文，就是每一个字後面。但是拼音把声调符号放在一个韵母上头，不在字尾。

1(So)–" ^ ", 2(MiSo)–" / ", 3(Do)–" v ",
4(SoDo)–" \ " and 5(Re)–" - ".

音标符号

B (ㄅㄆㄇㄈ), P (Pinyin), A (APA)

B	ㄅ	ㄆ	ㄇ	ㄈ		ㄉ	ㄊ	ㄋ	ㄌ
P	b	p	m	f		d	t	n	l
A	b	p	m	f		d	t	n	l

B	ㄍ	ㄎ	ㄏ		(ㄐ	ㄑ	ㄒ)		
P	g	k	h		(j	q	x)		
A	g	k	h		(dsi	tsi	si)		

B	ㄓ	ㄔ	ㄕ	ㄖ		ㄗ	ㄘ	ㄙ	
P	zh	ch	sh	r	z	c	s		
A	dR	tR	sR	R		ds	ts	s	

B	ㄚ	ㄛ	ㄜ	ㄝ		ㄞ	ㄟ	ㄠ	ㄡ
P	a	o	e	e		ai	ei	ao	ou
A	a	o	E	e		ai	ei	au	ou

B	(ㄢ)	ㄣ	(ㄤ)	ㄥ	ㄦ	ㄧ	ㄨ	ㄩ
P	(an)	n	(ang)	ng	er	yi	wu	ü
A	(an)	n	(ang)	ng	ER	yi	wu	yu

英文单字:	cup	hit	book	cat	very	red	zoo	you
发因字母	u	i	oo	a	v	r	z	you
APA 字母	A	I	U	ae	v	r	z	iu

52

英文单字:	judge	church	ship	vision	this	thin
发因字母	j	ch	sh	s	th	th
APA 字母	dZ	tZ	sZ	Z	D	T

＊声调符号

	1	2	3	4	5	6	7
Bopomofo		/	v	\			
Pinyin	-	/	v	\			
APA	^	/	v	\	-	v-	>
参考音高	Mi	ReMi	Do	MiDo	Do#	DoDo#	Re
大声音高	So	MiSo	Do	SoDo	Re	DoRe	Mi

I-3. Sample

For these four pages only, I will usc

for　DIz　for　peidZs　on^ll　ai　wll　iuz

APA phonetic symbols to mark the

a^pa　fo-ne^tlk　slm^bEls　tU　mark　DE

pronunciation of both English and

prE-nAn-sI-ei^Zen　Ef　boT　Ing^gllZ　End

Chinese sentences. In the foreword of

tZai-niz^　sen^tEns-Es In　DE　for^wErd　Ef

53

the book 'State of the World 2014,
DE bUk steit Ef DE wErld twen^tI for^tIn

Governing for Sustainability' author
ga^vErn-nIng for sEs-tein>E-bI^lI-tI o^Der

gave the whole world a hint of hope.
geiv DE hol wErld E hInt Ef hop

样本

只 在 这 四 页, 我 会 用 APA
dRv dsai\ dRE\ si\ ye\ wov hwei\ yong\ a^pa

音标 去 标 注 英 文 句 子 和
in^ byau^ tsyu\ byau^dRu\ ing^ wn/ dsyu\ ds- hE/

中 文 句 子。在 '2014 年 世界
dRong^wn/ dsyu\ ds- dsai\ ER\ling/ling/s\ nyen/sR\dsye\

现 况 报告,永续 管理' 一书
syen\kwang\ bau\gau\ yongvsyu\ gwan/liv i^ sRu^

的序言,作 者 给了全 世界
dE-syu\ yen/ dswo\dREv geiv IE- tsyuen/ sR\dsye\

一丝希望。
i^ s^ si^ wang\

54

It states "A different pattern has
It steits E dI^fE-rEnt pae^tErn haez

emerged in China, which joins
I-mEr^dZd In tZai^na (h)wItZ dZoinz

capitalism and authoritarian
kae^pI-to-IIzm End E-Do>rE-te^rIEn

government. ···It remains to be seen
gA^vErn-mnt It rI-meinz tE bi sin

whether the marriage of
(h)we^DE DE mae^rIEdZ

authoritarianism and public
Ef E-Do>rI-tei^rIE-nIzm En pA^bIIk

engagement can work over the long
In-gei^dZmEnt ken wErk o^vEr DE long

term."
tErm

55

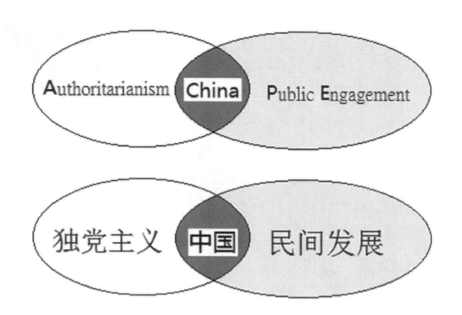

序言 说 "一個不同 的模式已在 中
syu\yen/sRwo^ i^   gE-bu\ tong/dE- mo/ sR\ iv dsai\dRong^

国 出现，它结 合了资本主 义和独
gwo/ tRu^syen\ ta^ dsye/ hE/ IE- ds^ bn/dRuv i\ hE/ du/

党政 府。···至於这个 独党 主 义 与
dangv dRng\fuv   dR\ yu/ dRE\ gE-du/ dangvdRuv i\ yuv

民间 发展 的婚 姻关 系能否长
min/dsyen^ fa^dRanv dE- hun^in^ gwan^ si^nng/ fov tRang/

久   维持下去 则 有 待观 察。"
dsyouv wei/tR/ sya\tsyu\dsE/youv dai\gwan^ tRa/

II. P132

In such a complicated world how could people find a common culture?

There is a Chinese saying,

"Live or die is all due to fate while be rich and noble is decided by heaven."

In ancient China people wished to establish three things before they passed away. The small one was to establish a good philosophy that might make people happy after people understood it. The middle one was to establish a sample of peaceful individuals by themselves, since as early of their lives as possible. The big one was to do something good to as many of others as possible. The good things normally could last for some limited period of time.

II-1. Detail of Principle 132

My idea is "one bag of three gems and two self-controls", named Principle 132, P132.

The three gems are Laozi's three treasures: be merciful, thrifty and yielding. The one bag is be diligent.

The two self-controls relate to "revenging" and "looking for win-win solution".

There are two kinds of revenge, one is try to live better than your foe/enemy and the other kind is try to make your foe/enemy sorrowful. You like to control yourself to stay on the first kind.

My suggestion on the second self-control is that, don't start working on a win-win solution if your ability or the timing is not there yet. You like to wait for the right timing while improving yourself.

II-2. 關於 13 品人， 2014

人是政事的主要因素所以必須知道人的根本．人有一正一副兩個根本，也就是情為正本而理為副本．情之為物，不只是在茲念茲而且要互感互益．古語說 "天下無不是的父母" 雖然誇張卻也暗示如果父母親不留意互感互益就容易被子女視為無情．想要互感互益那就需要 "理" 的協助，所以理為人之副本。聰者博記多理，智者遠見能清；明者了生知死，慧者總能雙贏。聰明可以勤耕，它，至死方休永無止境；智慧只能珍惜，它，可以欣賞不能強求。

情至少分為專博，長短，深淺，激緩和奇凡五種考量，各適雙方的天性，而 "合者有緣"。 正因為情之多采多姿，才能夠直教人生死相許．若論至情，非 "慈悲" 莫屬．所謂天地同慈一體大悲而物我兩忘再無是非，只有全心的慈悲。人之為物可以分為 3 等，每等大約 4 品，一共 13 品 (上下等，各分 4 品，中 5 品，一共 13 品) 的人格，介紹如下：

2-1. 至情至理，是明白知道相關客觀事實而全心慈悲的人。雖然這種知名的領袖不多，但是，有不少默默無聞的人，尤其是某些真喜歡做義工的人，卻是全心慈悲而且兼容至理，每天認真喜悅去過日子。他們當然是第一品人．世界因這些上等人而溫暖。絕大多數的第一品人是默默無名的。他們活在別人心中深處。

所謂知者不言言者不知，知道客觀事實的人不說，所以人們不知道他們知道。因此他們無名。

2-2. 至情足理，是明白超越事實，科學事實，個人事實，或宗教事實等等需要 "相信" 的事實，具有足理而全心慈悲的人，例如佛陀.

2-3. 足情至理，是明白相關客觀事實而全心利他，博愛，律己，或忠恕等等心中 "分別" 人我，具有足情的人，例如孔子和墨子.

2-4. 足情足理，是具有足情和足理的人，例如惠能，莊子和利他而不專利的居禮夫人.
2-4-1. 敝人主張雙悟，一悟今生，力求了解自性；一悟當下，力求不枉此生。在目前局勢中找一件有益人類的事，也就是盡心去做利他的事。

2-4-2. 如果天生智力或體力尚不足以照顧自己一身，只要盡力仍然有機會成為第4品人。 因為相關的個人事實很少所以仍可能足理，而全心徹底的律己也可能同時足情。只要用心認真的做，日子久了就見成績。

2-5. 足理有情，是至理或足理，有情而不足情的人，例如至理老子，解難曾參，解爭子思，本草天王李時珍，數學王子高斯，和台灣之光李遠哲.

2-6. 足情有理，是至情或足情，有理而不足理的人，例如至情證嚴上人，足情(利他領袖)孟子，王守仁，和岳飛，(律己領袖) 王陽明，和聖嚴法師。如果要能夠滿足信徒的情，情又那般多元化，所以信徒越多越難辦妥

2-7. 有情有理，是一般平凡可愛的人. 例如劉德華，張飛，費玉清，恆述法師，和蕭麗紅. 世界因這些至少 7 品的人而可喜有趣.

2-8. 有情弱理，是偶而失控或固執偏見的人.

2-9. 有理薄情，是比較自私的人.

2-10. 薄情弱理，是比較自私又偶而失控或固執偏見的人.

2-11. 薄情無理，是容易失控的人(真的瘋子).

2-12. 弱理無情，是完全自私的人(假裝是瘋子的人).

2-13. 無情無理，是完全自私又容易失控的人(弄假成真的瘋子)。

61

母親節是西方傳入台灣的好文化．由於母親的生活中心就是家庭，母親最關切的就是自己的子女，所以我認為，母親至少已經擁有 20%的天生利他真情．在 100 年前，父親必須把心思放在家庭以外的世界，所以關切子女的程度不及母親，大約不到一半，只有 8%的天生利他真情．雖然如今母親也須要賺錢，一般而言，父親卻長進不多，我的主觀評估，對有長進肯分工的父親，勉強給個 12%利他真情．然而，真心領養小孩的父母，又不一樣，真心的養父母各有 50%的利他真情．

我選幾位認識或深或淺的母親，試著分析她們的人品如下：

1.我太太二姊的婆家，她最近因癌症逝世．她知己甚明，眼光清澈，明白 100% 個人事實；在言行上律己甚嚴，只有朋友沒有敵人．享年近 90 歲，是足理足情第 4 品人．

2．我的丈母娘，過世多年．她的照片就在我放麥片熱飲的櫃子上．她領養一個親戚的小男孩，既有 50%的利他真情，又有 50%的律己表現，她是足情有理的第 6 品人．我太太的 50%利他真情表現於工作熱忱，頻頻領取服務獎，所以有其母必有其女，目前我太太已經是坐穩第 6 品，仍可提升

3．我的母親，有情有理，既有 20%的利他真情，又有 50%的律己表現，坐 7 望 6．有子不肖如我，私情稍微放縱。 而今的我，只得坐 9 望 7 的人品

4．我的二妹，有情有理，既有 20%的利他真情，又有 50%的律己表現；她發表許多論文，可惜我只讀過一篇，不確定她在理字的成就，所以我認為她可能是坐 7 或坐 5 而望 4．

5．我太太的同學，陳郁惠，既有 20%的利他真情，又有 50%的律己表現。她在 2012 年 7 月發現自己居然已經是癌症末期。她決定不進醫院，照常上班。她採用自然療法，工作到 2014 年 5 月，才在 8 月 26 日上午 9 點過世。郁惠非常瀟灑聰慧。是一個 4 品或 4 品以上的人。

6..最後要介紹的一位是我的朋友，Judy Fu，傅太太。

她 1972 年到美國東岸，已有一男一女．既有 20%的利他真情， 又有 50%的律己表現。然而，她可不簡單。她十分明白自己喜愛的人生是要在廚藝有所發展，而且，她到了美國就實際研習美國人的口味。在東岸入美以後，她進入餐飲業，大致了解經營方式；然後選擇西雅圖為目標市場。

搬到西雅圖，她在不同的餐廳掌廚，熟悉各地方的客人口味，終於在 1993 年開業。我在 1995 年認識她，她是我的主要客戶之一。 由於經常送錄影帶到她的 Snappy Dragon，所以對她店門外的特殊景像印象深刻。我發現總是有或多或少，在門外愉悅閒聊，耐心等候座位的客人。

她的客人大多是美國人，攜家帶眷的多，成雙的也有．她的麵食口碑極佳，西雅圖時報經常票選她的 Snappy Dragon 為四星級餐館。

在她的餐館工作，即使是不景氣的時期也完全不受裁員威脅。 既然長久以來提供許多人 "美好麵食"，我認為 100% 的利他真情對 Judy 來說是當仁不讓。

她現在已經 74 歲，仍然每天工作 4 小時以上，樂此不疲。她又完全明白個人事實，樂在其中；她是坐 4 望 3，也許，是望 1 的人品呢。

What I say & do today,
decide my future & define me.

今日的言行，造就明日的我。

What I say & do today,
decide my future & define me.

今日的言行，造就明日的我。

What I say & do today,
decide my future & define me.

今日的言行，造就明日的我。

What I say & do today,
decide my future & define me.

今日的言行，造就明日的我。

What I say & do today,
decide my future & define me.

今日的言行，造就明日的我。